DATE DUE

AUG 2 8 2009			
GAYLORD			PRINTED IN U.S.A.

DEC 3 , 2005

California

AMERICAN

REGIONAL COOKING
LIBRARY
Culture, Tradition,
and History

African American
American Indian
Amish and Mennonite
California
Hawaiian
Louisiana
Mexican American
Mid-Atlantic
Midwest
New England
Northwest
Southern
Southern Appalachian
Texas
Thanksgiving

California

Mason Crest Publishers

Philadelphia

Mason Crest Publishers Inc.
370 Reed Road
Broomall, Pennsylvania 19008
(866) MCP-BOOK (toll free)
www.masoncrest.com

First printing
1 2 3 4 5 6 7 8 9 10

Library of Congress Cataloging-in-Publication Data

Libal, Joyce.
  California / Joyce Libal.
      p. cm. — (American regional cooking library)
  Includes index.
  ISBN 1-59084-613-3
  1. Cookery, American—California style—Juvenile literature. I. Title. II. Series.
  TX715.2.C34L53 2005
  641.59794—dc22
                                    2004007579
Compiled by Joyce Libal.
Recipes by Patricia Therrien.
Recipes tested and prepared by Bonni Phelps.
Produced by Harding House Publishing Services, Inc., Vestal, New York.
Interior design by Dianne Hodack.
Cover design by Michelle Bouch.
Printed and bound in the Hashemite Kingdom of Jordan.

Contents

Introduction
by the Culinary Institute of America

Cooking is a dynamic profession, one that presents some of the greatest challenges and offers some of the greatest rewards. Since 1946, the Culinary Institute of America has provided aspiring and seasoned food service professionals with the knowledge and skills needed to become leaders and innovators in this industry.

Here at the CIA, we teach our students the fundamental culinary techniques they need to build a sound foundation for their food service careers. There is always another level of perfection for them to achieve and another skill to master. Our rigorous curriculum provides them with a springboard to continued growth and success.

Food is far more than simply sustenance or the source of energy to fuel you and your family through life's daily regimen. It conjures memories throughout life, summoning up the smell, taste, and flavor of simpler times. Cooking is more than an art and a science; it provides family history. Food prepared with care epitomizes the love, devotion, and culinary delights that you offer to your friends and family.

A cuisine provides a way to express and establish customs—the way a food should taste and the flavors and aromas associated with that food. Cuisines are more than just a collection of ingredients, cooking utensils, and dishes from a geographic location; they are elements that are critical to establishing a culinary identity.

When you can accurately read a recipe, you can trace a variety of influences by observing which ingredients are selected and also by noting the technique that is used. If you research the historical origins of a recipe, you may find ingredients that traveled from East to West or from the New World to the Old. Traditional methods of cooking a dish may have changed with the times or to meet special challenges.

The history of cooking illustrates the significance of innovation and the trading or sharing of ingredients and tools between societies. Although the various cooking vessels over the years have changed, the basic cooking methods have remained the same. Through adaptation, a recipe created years ago in a remote corner of the world could today be recognized by many throughout the globe.

When observing the customs of different societies, it becomes apparent that food brings people together. It is the common thread that we share and that we value. Regardless of the occasion, food is present to celebrate and to comfort. Through food we can experience other cultures and lands, learning the significance of particular ingredients and cooking techniques.

As you begin your journey through the culinary arts, keep in mind the power that food and cuisine holds. When passed from generation to generation, family heritage and traditions remain strong. Become familiar with the dishes your family has enjoyed through the years and play a role in keeping them alive. Don't be afraid to embellish recipes along the way – creativity is what cooking is all about.

California Culture, History, and Traditions

Today California is a true "melting pot" of culture and cuisine. To find out how it got that way, we need only take a quick look at its geography and history.

Stretching from Oregon on the north to Mexico on the south, this long, narrow state is blessed with an immense expanse of Pacific Ocean coastline. More than a hundred different Indian groups were already living in the area when Spanish explorers, who first arrived on the Baja coast in 1535, named the land after a treasure island in one of their romantic folk tales.

"California" is a fitting name as the ocean offers "treasure" in the form of abundant seafood and the climate is such that fresh fruits and vegetables can be grown throughout the year. The Europeans brought seeds and agricultural techniques that made cultivation of many fruits and vegetables possible and changed the face of California forever. Those who settled here combined a multitude of local ingredients with their own diverse cooking heritage. Influences from Europe, Asia, Central and South America, and the Caribbean are all evident in today's creative California cuisine.

Think of California, and you think of surfers on the beach, people skating on busy sidewalks, and skiers rocketing down mountain slopes. The people of this state have a health-conscious tradition that they've translated into a lean diet based on unique and flavorful foods. Fresh, locally grown fruits, vegetables, nuts, and herbs, and high quality meat, seafood, and dairy products are readily available to California cooks who have a knack for combining the best of their culinary traditions with innovative new foods as they become available. "California fusion" is a term used to describe the energy of this "marriage" of multiple cooking styles with diverse and abundant fresh ingredients.

Of course the state that ships so much fresh produce to the rest of the country has lush and tantalizing food choices available to its own residents. More recent immigration has added Thai food and Vietnamese cuisine to the eclectic mix. Some of the best

The Golden Gate Bridge in San Francisco, California.

restaurants in the United States are located in California and, perhaps because of the sophisticated and glamorous population that resides there, the food has a beautiful and stylish presentation.

Modern shipping methods now make it possible for you to experiment with "California fusion" in your own kitchen. You'll find 20 recipes in this book to help you get started.

Before you cook...

If you haven't done much cooking before, you may find recipe books a little confusing. Certain words and terms can seem unfamiliar. You may find the measurements difficult to understand. What appears to be an easy or familiar dish may contain ingredients you've never heard of before. You might not understand what utensil the recipe calls for you to use, or you might not be sure what the recipe is asking you to do.

Reading the pages in this section before you get started may help you understand the directions better so that your cooking goes more smoothly. You can also refer back to these pages whenever you run into questions.

Safety Tips

Cooking involves handling very hot and very sharp objects, so being careful is common sense. What's more, you want to be certain that anything you plan on putting in your mouth is safe to eat. If you follow these easy tips, you should find that cooking can be both fun and safe.

Trees in California's redwood forest

Before you cook...

- Always wash your hands before and after handling food. This is particularly important after you handle raw meats, poultry, and eggs, as bacteria called salmonella can live on these uncooked foods. You can't see or smell salmonella, but these germs can make you or anyone who swallows them very sick.
- Make a habit of using potholders or oven mitts whenever you handle pots and pans from the oven or microwave.
- Always set pots, pans, and knives with their handles away from counter edges. This way you won't risk catching your sleeves on them—and any younger children in the house won't be in danger of grabbing something hot or sharp.
- Don't leave perishable food sitting out of the refrigerator for more than an hour or two.
- Wash all raw fruits and vegetables to remove dirt and chemicals.
- Use a cutting board when chopping vegetables or fruit, and always cut away from yourself.
- Don't overheat grease or oil—but if grease or oil does catch fire, don't try to extinguish the flames with water. Instead, throw baking soda or salt on the fire to put it out. Turn all stove burners off.
- If you burn yourself, immediately put the burn under cold water, as this will prevent the burn from becoming more painful.
- Never put metal dishes or utensils in the microwave. Use only microwave-proof dishes.
- Wash cutting boards and knives thoroughly after cutting meat, fish or poultry — especially when raw and before using the same tools to prepare other foods such as vegetables and cheese. This will prevent the spread of bacteria such as salmonella.
- Keep your hands away from any moving parts of appliances, such as mixers.
- Unplug any appliance, such as a mixer, blender, or food processor before assembling for use or disassembling after use.

Metric Conversion Table

Most cooks in the United States use measuring containers based on an eight-ounce cup, a teaspoon, and a tablespoon. Meanwhile, cooks in Canada and Europe are more apt to use metric measurements. The recipes in this book use cups, teaspoons, and tablespoons—but you can convert these measurements to metric by using the table below.

Temperature
To convert Fahrenheit degrees to Celsius, subtract 32 and multiply by .56.

212ºF = 100ºC
(this is the boiling point of water)
250ºF = 110ºC
275ºF = 135ºC
300ºF = 150ºC
325ºF = 160ºC
350ºF = 180ºC
375ºF = 190ºC
400ºF = 200ºC

Liquid Measurements
1 teaspoon = 5 milliliters
1 tablespoon = 15 milliliters
1 fluid ounce = 30 milliliters
1 cup = 240 milliliters
1 pint = 480 milliliters
1 quart = 0.95 liters
1 gallon = 3.8 liters

Measurements of Mass or Weight
1 ounce = 28 grams
8 ounces = 227 grams
1 pound (16 ounces) = 0.45 kilograms
2.2 pounds = 1 kilogram

Measurements of Length
¼ inch = 0.6 centimeters
½ inch = 1.25 centimeters
1 inch = 2.5 centimeters

Pan Sizes

Baking pans are usually made in standard sizes. The pans used in the United States are roughly equivalent to the following metric pans:

9-inch cake pan = 23-centimeter pan
11x7-inch baking pan = 28x18-centimeter baking pan
13x9-inch baking pan = 32.5x23-centimeter baking pan
9x5-inch loaf pan = 23x13-centimeter loaf pan
2-quart casserole = 2-liter casserole

Useful Tools, Utensils, Dishes

basting brush

blender

Dutch oven

bundt pan

food processor

garlic press

jelly roll pan

pastry cutter

pepper mill

rubber spatula

serrated knife

skillet

sushi mat

vegetable scrub brush

vegetable peeler

vegetable steamer

wire whisk

wok

Cooking Glossary

cream A term used to describe mixing sugar with butter or shortening until they are light and well blended.

cut Mix solid shortening or butter into flour, usually by using a pastry blender or two knives and making short, chopping strokes until the mixture looks like small pellets.

dash Just a couple of drops.

dollop A small mound, about 1 or 2 tablespoons.

dredge To coat meat or seafood with flour or crumbs usually by dragging or tossing.

fold Gently combining a lighter substance with a heavier batter by spooning the lighter mixture through the heavier one without using strong beating strokes.

hulled A seed that has had the hard, outer covering removed.

minced Cut into very small pieces.

sauté Fry in a skillet or wok over high heat while stirring.

shucked Seafood (such as oysters, clams, or mussels) with the shell removed.

steam To cook over just a small amount of boiling water.

tapioca A granular preparation of cassava starch used as a thickener.

toss Turn food over quickly and lightly so that it is evenly covered with a liquid or powder.

Special California Flavors

avocados

balsamic, rice, wine vinegars

basil

cilantro

chilies

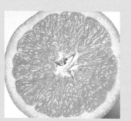

lemons

limes

salsa

California Recipes

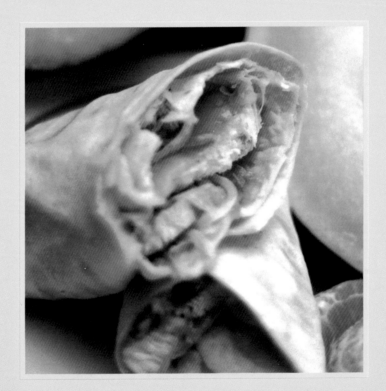

Glazed Granola

This hearty cereal is yummy any time of the day or night.

Preheat oven to 300° Fahrenheit.

Ingredients:

2 cups old-fashioned or quick-cooking oats, uncooked
½ cup hulled sunflower seeds
¼ cup slivered almonds
½ cup wheat germ
1 cup shredded coconut
½ cup butter or margarine
¼ cup honey
½ teaspoon salt
2 cups raisins

Cooking utensils you'll need:
small sauce pan
large mixing bowl
measuring cups
measuring spoons
jelly roll pan

Directions:

Measure and pour the oats, sunflower seeds, almonds, wheat germ, and coconut into the mixing bowl, and stir them together. Melt the butter in the saucepan and mix in honey and salt. Pour the warm liquid over the dry ingredients, and stir well. Spread the mixture on a greased jelly roll pan, and place it in the oven. Remove the pan from the oven several times while the granola is baking, and stir the mixture. Bake until golden brown (usually about 30 minutes). While the granola is still hot, stir in the raisins. When the granola is cool, store it in a tightly covered container in the refrigerator.

Tip:

Use any nuts and dried fruits that you enjoy to custom design this cereal to your personal taste, and eat it with milk, yogurt, or as a dry snack.

California Food History

Spanish missionaries first began moving from Mexico to California in the 1700s, bringing grapevines with them. By the mid-1850s, Egyptian Muscat grapes were being grown near San Diego. This area was not ideal for grapes, however, and farmers soon moved them into the San Joaquin (pronounced "wah keen") Valley. According to legend, a heat wave that occurred before the grape harvest of 1873 produced the first raisins by causing the grapes to dry on the vines. In 1876, William Thompson, a Scottish immigrant, produced a seedless grape that was sweet and tasty. Additionally, it had a thin skin, making it well suited for drying. Today, Thompson Seedless Grapes account for approximately 95 percent of the raisins grown in California, and the San Joaquin Valley is the world's largest producer of grapes.

Hangtown Fry

First made in the late 1800s in gold-mining camps, this one-skillet meal is sometimes credited as being the first California cuisine.

Ingredients:

3 eggs
1 tablespoon milk
3 shucked oysters
2 slices bacon
1/2 cup cracker crumbs
1/2 cup dry bread crumbs
cooking oil

Cooking utensils you'll need:
3 small mixing bowls
2 skillets

Directions:

Mix the cracker crumbs and bread crumbs together in one bowl and set aside. Mix one egg with the milk in another bowl and set aside. Begin cooking the bacon in one of the skillets over medium heat. While it is cooking, wash the oysters and pat them dry with paper towels. Dip the oysters in the egg mixture and then dredge them in the crumbs. Put a little cooking oil in the second skillet and fry the oysters until they are almost done (approximately 5 minutes). While they are cooking, beat 2 eggs lightly in the remaining bowl. When the bacon is almost crisp arrange the slices close together and pour about half of the beaten eggs over them. Put the fried oysters on top of the bacon and pour the remaining eggs on top. Continue cooking until the eggs are done, and fold the omelet in half.

Tips:

You can purchase crumbs, but it's easy to make both bread and cracker crumbs in a food processor. If you don't have a food processor, you can make cracker crumbs neatly by placing crackers in a plastic bag and crushing them with a rolling pin.

An easy way to dredge the oysters is to place the bread and cracker crumb mixture in a paper bag, add the oysters, and shake.

California Food History

Placerville, California, was known as Hangtown in the 1800s. Today's Cary House Hotel was then the site of the El Dorado Hotel where, according to legend, Hangtown Fry was developed before the mid 1800s. At that time an order of Hangtown Fry cost about $6.00. That might not sound like much now, but it was an extremely expensive meal in those days. The high cost was due to the fact that live oysters had to be transported in barrels of seawater all the way from San Francisco. Men from gold-mining camps ordered Hangtown Fry as a way of celebrating when they "struck it rich." By the mid 1800s, Hangtown Fry was famous and could be obtained across the entire Northwest Territory.

Energy in a Glass

Instead of soda, treat yourself to this tasty after-school-pick-me-up!

Ingredients:

2 cups orange juice
2 tablespoons lemon juice
1 banana
1 cup cantaloupe or watermelon
1 carrot
8 ice cubes

Cooking utensils you'll need:
blender
paring knife
vegetable peeler or vegetable scrub brush

Directions:

Peel the fruits and cut them into chunks. Peel the carrot with the vegetable peeler, if desired, and cut it into small pieces. (If you don't wish to peel the carrot, be sure to scrub it very well with a brush.) Place the juices, fruits, and carrot in a blender. Cover and blend at high speed or liquify for about a minute. Add the ice cubes and blend again until thick and frothy.

Tip:

You can make smoothies like this one using any of your favorite fruits. Add a little yogurt for a protein boost.

California Fruit Salad

Ingredients:

½ cantaloupe
½ honeydew melon
⅛ small watermelon
1 banana
1 kiwi
¼ cup raisins
¼ cup walnuts
8 ounces plain or vanilla lowfat yogurt
1¼ teaspoons cinnamon

Cooking utensils you'll need:
large mixing bowl
slicing knife
measuring cups
measuring spoons

Directions:

Peel and cut the melons, banana, and kiwi into bite-sized chunks and place them in the bowl. Mix in the raisins and nuts. Blend the cinnamon into the yogurt, pour over the fruit, and stir.

Tip:

You can also serve the cinnamon/yogurt dressing on the side and dip the fruit chunks into it.

California Food History

More walnuts are grown on the west coast than anywhere else in the world. Even though only 15 percent of California is under cultivation, it produces more agricultural products than any other state.

Mesclun Salad

This food might sound unfamiliar, but you have probably eaten it many times. Mesclun is simply a mixture of small, young salad greens. It is available in most supermarkets under a variety of names including spring mix, salad mix, and gourmet salad mix. The delicious potpourri can include the leaves of many different vegetables such as radicchio, oak leaf lettuce, dandelion, arugula, spinach, beet greens, fresée, sorrel, and mizuma.

Ingredients:

3 cups mesclun
1 chopped shallot
1 garlic clove
2 tablespoons red wine vinegar
1 tablespoon balsamic vinegar
1 teaspoon Dijon mustard
½ cup extra virgin olive oil

Cooking utensils you'll need:
wooden salad bowl
measuring cups
measuring spoons

Directions:

Peel the garlic and use it to rub the interior of the salad bowl. (This will impart a subtle garlic flavor to the salad.) Pour the red wine vinegar and balsamic vinegar into the salad bowl. Stir in the shallot and mustard. Pour in the olive oil and mix well. Add the mesclun and toss your salad.

Tips:

All olive oils are not equal. Extra virgin olive oil has the most intense flavor because it comes from the first cold pressing of the olives and does not involve any chemical processing. Extra virgin olive oil is a healthy food for many reasons: it helps to satisfy hunger so fewer calories may be eaten at the meal, it helps protect against cardio-vascular disease, and it may help prevent some cancers.

Vinegar comes in many different flavors. Red wine vinegar has a bold, full-bodied taste while balsamic vinegar is mellow with a sweet and sour tang.

America's Salad Bowl

Franciscan missionaries were the ones who first planted olive groves in California. In fact, some of the trees in today's groves are as old as 150 years.

California has more than 75,000 farms and they supply over half of the produce now eaten in the United States. So much lettuce is produced in California that it is sometimes referred to as the salad bowl of America.

Much of the garlic used in the United States comes from California, and each year the town of Gilroy celebrates the pungent cloves in a big way. You can taste almost anything made with garlic at the annual event—even ice cream!

Ceasar Salad

Raw eggs are a traditional ingredient in Ceasar Salad Dressing. Nowadays we need to be concerned about the possibility of getting salmonella from raw eggs, so that ingredient has been eliminated from this recipe.

Ingredients:

1 ounce anchovies, mashed to a paste
1 garlic clove
1 cup extra virgin olive oil
2 teaspoons Dijon mustard
2 tablespoons red wine vinegar
1 teaspoon Worcestershire sauce
salt
freshly ground black pepper
romaine lettuce
ripe olives
small red onion, thinly sliced
shredded Parmesan cheese
croutons

Cooking utensils you'll need:
mixing bowl or blender
measuring cups
measuring spoons
garlic press (optional)
pepper mill (optional)

Directions:

Mash the anchovies to a paste in the bowl or place them in a blender. Use a garlic press to squeeze the garlic onto the anchovies (or chop it first). Add the olive oil, mustard, wine vinegar, and Worcestershire sauce. Mix or blend and add salt and pepper to taste. Tear the romaine leaves into large pieces and place on serving plates or a salad bowl. Add olives and slivers of red onion. Top with dressing and shredded cheese. Add the croutons last so they stay crunchy.

Tips:

Canned anchovies and anchovy paste are available in the canned fish section of most supermarkets.

You can purchase croutons, but it's easy to make your own. Just cut bread into half-inch cubes. For 2 cups of bread cubes, place 2 tablespoons of olive oil in a bowl and add 1 tablespoon grated Parmesan cheese. Squeeze a little garlic into it, and quickly toss the bread around in the mixture. Spread the bread cubes on a jellyroll pan and bake in a preheated 375° Fahrenheit oven for about 15 to 20 minutes (until it is lightly browned). Turn the bread occasionally while baking.

California Food History

When food supplies ran low in the Cardini restaurant in Tijuana, Mexico, the Italian owner, Caesar Cardini, got creative. It is reported that he instructed his staff to, "Take everything to the table and make a ceremony of fixing the salad." He wanted customers to think that it was the house specialty, and that's exactly what it became. Hollywood stars who frequently ate at the restaurant loved the salad, and soon it was also a popular dish in the Los Angeles area. Later the International Society of Epicures in Paris voted it "the greatest recipe to originate in the Americas in fifty years." Today, it is a popular salad all across America.

Green Chile Chicken Soup

Ingredients:

2 cups cooked rice
1 cup cooked chicken breast, cut in cubes
4 cups chicken broth
vegetable cooking spray
⅓ cup sliced green onions
1 (10½-ounce) can diced tomatoes with green chiles, undrained
1 (4-ounce) can chopped green chiles, undrained
1 tablespoon lime juice
salt to taste
tortilla chips
½ cup chopped tomato
½ cup chopped avocado
4 lime slices
fresh cilantro

Cooking utensils you'll need:
Dutch oven or large saucepan with cover
rice cooker or small saucepan with cover
measuring cups
measuring spoons

Directions:

Cook rice according to package directions. While it is cooking, coat the bottom of the Dutch oven with vegetable spray. Add onions and cook over medium/high heat until tender. Stir in the chicken broth, canned tomatoes and canned chiles, chicken, and rice. Bring the soup to a simmer over medium/high heat, turn the heat down to low, cover, and cook 20 minutes. Add the lime juice and salt to taste just before serving. Ladle the soup into 4 bowls and top each serving with tortilla chips, chopped tomato and avocado, a lime slice, and fresh cilantro.

Tip:

You can use canned chicken broth for this recipe or boil raw chicken parts in water for a couple of hours to make your own.

California Food Facts

Rice is available in long-, medium-, and short-grain varieties. The type grown in California is medium-grain japonica, which is prized because it cooks to a soft and somewhat sticky consistency. Use it for soups, casseroles, risotto, or any time you desire a soft variety. Rice is a staple in the diets of more people in the world than any other food. It is an excellent source of complex carbohydrates (the "good carbs" that provide your body with energy) and also contains iron, thiamin, niacin, riboflavin, and potassium.

California Sunshine Soup

A cold soup that's as pretty as sunshine in a bowl.

Ingredients:

2½ cups orange juice
2 tablespoons sugar
2 tablespoons quick–cooking tapioca
dash of salt
2 cinnamon sticks
12 ounces frozen sliced peaches, thawed
1½ cups orange sections
1 banana
¼ cup sour cream

Cooking utensils you'll need:
saucepan
mixing bowl
measuring cups
measuring spoons

Directions:

Pour the orange juice in the saucepan and stir in the sugar, tapioca, and salt. Let stand for 5 minutes, place the cinnamon sticks in the mixture, and boil over medium heat for the amount of time listed on the tapioca package. Pour the mixture into the bowl and allow it to cool. Then remove cinnamon sticks and peel and slice the banana. Stir the "soup" and add the peaches, orange sections, and bananas. Chill well in the refrigerator and garnish each serving with a dollop of sour cream.

Tip:

Chill serving bowls before filling them with cold soup.

BLT and Avocado Sandwich

Creamy avocado adds extra texture and subtle, nutlike flavor to this favorite sandwich.

Ingredients:

2 slices bacon
2 slices whole wheat bread
1½ teaspoons Thousand Island dressing
1 tablespoon mayonnaise
lettuce (a mixture like mesclun is best)
tomato
avocado

Directions:

Place the bacon in the skillet and begin frying over medium heat. When it is crisp, place the bacon on a piece of paper towel to drain off some of the fat. While the bacon is still cooking, however, mix the salad dressing and mayonnaise together, and toast the bread. Spread the salad dressing mixture on the toast. Place the desired amount of lettuce on one of the toasted slices. Add thin slices of tomato, the crisp bacon, and slices of avocado. Top with the other slice of toast and enjoy.

Tips:

Although avocados can be firm when purchased, wait until they are somewhat soft to the touch before using them. Don't peel avocados until just before use because their beautiful yellow-green interior turns an unsightly brown very quickly. Coating cut surfaces with lemon juice helps to maintain the original color.

California Food Facts

Avocado trees were first planted the United States in 1830, and today approximately 80 percent of our annual avocado crop is grown in California. Although the main avocado crops peak in spring and summer, you can usually find them in supermarkets all year long. Several types are available, but the Haas is the most popular. Spring and summer varieties are usually smooth skinned while fall varieties are generally more pebbly and a darker green color.

California Food History

Mexico gained control of California in 1821 when it won independence from Spain. Gold was discovered in California and it became a United States territory in 1848 after the Mexican-American War, and in 1850 it became a state. These events opened the door to widespread immigration of people from many lands, but this region has never lost its Hispanic flavors. With Mexico just a drive south, Mexican foods are common dishes throughout California.

Mexican Chicken Wrap

Ingredients:

2 boneless, skinless chicken breasts
vegetable spray
½ teaspoon Mexican seasoning
three 12-inch flour tortillas
1 cup shredded Monterey Jack cheese with peppers
½ red onion, chopped
2 plum tomatoes, chopped
Ranch dressing
Salsa (mild, medium, or hot)

Directions:

Coat the bottom of the skillet with cooking spray. Cut each chicken breast into 6 or more slices, sprinkle them with the seasoning, and sauté for about 6 minutes (until thoroughly cooked) over medium/high heat. Remove chicken slices and set them aside. Put one tortilla in the skillet, top with ⅓ cup of the cheese, and cook for approximately 2 minutes. When the cheese is melted, remove the tortilla from the skillet, place another tortilla in the skillet and repeat the process. While the second tortilla is cooking, layer the first tortilla with ⅓ of the chicken slices, onion, and tomato, and 1 or 2 tablespoons of Ranch dressing. Roll the tortilla up, and repeat with the remaining ingredients. Serve each chicken wrap with a dollop of salsa on the side.

Tips:

No red onion? No problem. Use any onion that's available.

Look for Mexican seasoning with other dried seasoning or in the Mexican food section of your grocery store. You can also substitute other seasonings in this recipe.

Turkey Cobb Salad Sandwich

Ingredients:

8 ounces cooked turkey breast
6 slices bacon
4 slices pain de mie or other firm white bread
2 ounces blue cheese
2 tablespoons mayonnaise
1 avocado
4 leaves romaine lettuce

Cooking utensils you'll need:
skillet
toaster
paring knife

Directions:

Place bacon slices in the skillet and cook over medium heat until crisp. Drain the cooked bacon on paper towels to remove some of the fat. Slice the turkey breast diagonally into thin slices. Toast the bread. Peel the avocado and cut into thin slices. For each sandwich, spread one slice of toast with one tablespoon of mayonnaise. Spread the second slice of toast with half of the blue cheese and top with half of the turkey, bacon, avocado slices, and lettuce. Place the first slice of bread on top and serve.

Tips:

Cooked turkey breast is available in the deli section of most supermarkets. You can also purchase fresh or frozen turkey breast and cook it according to the directions on the package.

History of Cobb Salad

This world-famous salad was invented in the 1920s by Rob Cobb, then manager of Hollywood's Brown Derby restaurant. According to legend, a group of movie executives walked into the restaurant. Apparently the restaurant was running low on certain salad ingredients, so Mr. Cobb made his namesake salad out of all the leftovers in the refrigerator.

41

Herbed Tomato Slices with Feta

If you want to be healthy, eat tomatoes! They're loaded with lycopene, an important antioxidant. Antioxidants help to counteract free radicals, the "bad guys" that contribute to many illnesses including heart disease and cancer.

Ingredients:

2 tomatoes
½ cup crumbled feta cheese
2 tablespoons balsamic vinegar
3 tablespoons extra virgin olive oil
2 tablespoons canola oil
1 teaspoon mustard
salt to taste
freshly ground black pepper to taste
fresh parsley, chopped
fresh basil, cut in strips
fresh chives, minced

Cooking utensils you'll need:
serrated knife
measuring spoons
small mixing bowl
wire whisk
plate
pepper mill (optional)

Directions:

Cut each tomato in half, remove the seeds, and place the tomatoes on a plate with their cut sides down to drain. Pour the vinegar, oils, and mustard in a bowl and whisk, adding salt and pepper to taste. Turn the tomato halves cut side up and top each with a tablespoon of feta cheese and basil strips. Sprinkle with parsley and chives and drizzle the dressing over everything.

Tips:

It's easier to cut tomatoes using a knife with a serrated edge than with a smooth-edged knife.

For this recipe, you can use any type of cheese that suits your fancy. You can also vary the flavor of the dressing by substituting different types of mustard (such as green-peppercorn or hot and spicy mustard).

California Food Facts

More lycopene is available in processed tomatoes than in fresh
ones, so be sure to include tomato juice and sauce in your diet.
Even ketchup is a good source of lycopene! You can boost the
lycopene in this recipe by baking the tomatoes and cheese in
the oven before adding the herbs and dressing.

Sushi

This popular food originated in Japan. There are many different types of sushi, but basically it consists of seafood and vegetables rolled in rice and edible varieties of seaweed. Most sushi contains raw saltwater fish. Professional sushi chefs are trained to recognize suitable fish and to make certain the fish are free of parasites. The recipe below is for vegetarian sushi.

Ingredients:

1½ cups sushi rice (short-grain rice or medium-grain pearl rice)
2½ cups water
¼ cup rice vinegar
3 tablespoons sugar
½ teaspoon salt
1 cucumber
1 carrot
1 tablespoon water
1 avocado
nori (see Tips)
soy sauce
wasabi (green horseradish paste)

Cooking utensils you'll need:
rice cooker or saucepan with cover
microwave
microwave-safe dish
mixing bowl
measuring cups
measuring spoons
sushi mat
waxed paper

Directions:

Bring the rice and 2½ cups water to a boil, cover, reduce heat and simmer until the water is absorbed (usually about 15 to 20 minutes). Meanwhile, mix together the rice vinegar, sugar, and salt. Taste and adjust ingredients as desired. Add mixture to the cooked rice and set aside to cool. Peel and cut the cucumber, carrot, and avocado into long, thin strips. Microwave the carrot in 1 tablespoon water for 2 or 3 minutes.

Place a sheet of nori on a sushi mat. Spread 1 cup of rice on the nori, but leave about 2 inches at one end of the nori free of rice. Place vegetable and avocado strips together in one row along the middle of the rice. Lift the mat carefully as you roll the sushi, squeeze the mat gently to secure the sushi roll ingredients, and gently unroll the mat. Wrap the sushi roll in waxed paper, set it aside, and make another. Slice sushi rolls about 1-inch thick and serve with soy sauce and wasabi.

Tips:

Nori is an edible seaweed that is available in ready-to-use sheets.

If you'd like to make sushi with seafood, cook a small amount of shrimp in boiling water. Then cool, peel, slice, and add to the vegetables in this sushi recipe.

California Food History

The first groups of settlers that came from Japan to the United States arrived in California in 1869. These first immigrants brought mulberry trees, silk cocoons, tea plants, bamboo roots, and other agricultural products. The U.S. Census of 1870 showed fifty-five Japanese in the United States; thirty-three lived in California. By 1880, the Census showed eighty-six Japanese in California, with a total of 148 in the United States. Many Japanese moved to Hawaii, and then went on to the United States mainland. In 1890, 2,038 Japanese resided in the United States; of this number, 1,114 lived in California, and the numbers have continued to grow since then. Japanese Americans have added their own unique dishes to the wide variety of California foods.

California Stir-Fry

Ingredients:

¾ pound fresh asparagus
¾ cup chicken broth
1 tablespoon cornstarch
1 teaspoon soy sauce
1 teaspoon sesame oil
¾ pound sea scallops
1 carrot
1 tablespoon water
1 avocado
nori (see Tips p. 47)
soy sauce
wasabi (green horseradish paste)

Cooking utensils you'll need:
rice cooker or saucepan with cover
vegetable steamer or saucepan with cover
wok or large skillet
paring knife
garlic press
small mixing bowl
measuring cups
measuring spoons

Directions:

Break the tough bottom off of each asparagus spear and discard. (As you put pressure on the bottom of the spear, it will make a natural break between the tender, edible portion and the rest.) Use a paring knife to remove any tough scales from the stems, and wash the asparagus spears. Steam just until the spears are crisp/tender (3 to 5 minutes). Drain, run under cold water to stop the cooking process, drain again, and set aside.

Cook the rice according to package directions. While it's cooking, pour the chicken broth into the mixing bowl. Add soy sauce and cornstarch, stir briskly, and set aside.

Wash the scallops and pat them dry with paper towels. Cut each scallop in half. Pour the sesame oil into the wok or skillet and begin to heat. Add the scallops and mushrooms and use the garlic press to squeeze the garlic into the wok. Stir-fry just until the scallops are cooked (about 4 minutes). Add the chicken-stock mixture and continue to cook until the sauce begins to thicken. Add the cherry tomatoes, green onions, and asparagus. Continue stir-frying until all vegetables are hot, add salt and pepper to taste, and serve over hot rice.

Tips:

You can use canned chicken broth for this recipe or boil raw chicken parts in water for a couple of hours to make your own.

If you don't have a garlic press, mince the garlic.

You can quickly slice mushrooms using an egg slicer.

California Food History

The first groups of settlers that came from Japan to the United States arrived in California in 1869. These first immigrants brought mulberry trees, silk cocoons, tea plants, bamboo roots, and other agricultural products. The U.S. Census of 1870 showed fifty-five Japanese in the United States; thirty-three lived in California. By 1880, the Census showed eighty-six Japanese in California, with a total of 148 in the United States. Many Japanese moved to Hawaii, and then went on to the United States mainland. In 1890, 2,038 Japanese resided in the United States; of this number, 1,114 lived in California, and the numbers have continued to grow since then. Japanese Americans have added their own unique dishes to the wide variety of California foods.

Stacked Salmon

Preheat oven to 450° Fahrenheit.

Ingredients:

two 1- to 1½-inch thick salmon steaks
½ pound small shrimp, shelled and cleaned
extra virgin olive oil
½ pound sliced button mushrooms
½ pint sour cream
½ teaspoon tarragon
salt
freshly ground pepper

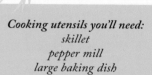

Cooking utensils you'll need:
skillet
pepper mill
large baking dish

Directions:

Wash fish and shrimp and pat dry with paper towels. Place 2 tablespoons of olive oil in the skillet, sauté the mushrooms until tender, add the shrimp and continue to sauté for another minute. Grease the bottom of the baking dish with olive oil. Place one of the salmon steaks in the pan and brush with additional olive oil. Spread the cooked shrimp/mushroom mixture on the oiled salmon, sprinkle with a little salt and pepper, and place the remaining salmon steak on top. Mix the tarragon into the sour cream. Pour the sour cream over the salmon and bake for approximately 20 minutes (until the fish flakes easily with a fork).

Tips:

If you're concerned about the amount of fat in your diet, substitute low-fat or nonfat sour cream for the regular variety in recipes.

Use portabello mushrooms instead of the button mushrooms to add a meaty flavor to this dish.

California Food History

During colonial times, salmon was abundant in America on both the east and west coasts. Many American Indian people depended heavily upon this large, pink fish. In fact, the Chinook people feared starvation without it and developed a ritual around its consumption—to appease the spirit of the salmon whenever it was eaten, the heart was burnt to protect it from consumption by wild animals or dogs. The canning of salmon began in New England in 1864, and the salmon population along the Atlantic coast of the United States was soon destroyed. California began supplying the eastern United States with canned salmon in 1864. Although salmon is still available from the Pacific Ocean, all Atlantic salmon now comes from Canada or Europe.

Salmon live in saltwater but migrate inland to freshwater to spawn (lay their eggs). Today salmon are also raised on fish farms, but these fish are not as flavorful as the wild variety. Salmon is pink because of the astaxanthin (a pigment) contained in the crustaceans and insects that are its food source. Salmon is an important source of antioxidants, and many health professionals recommend we eat it regularly.

Artichoke and Ham Fettuccini

Ingredients:

4 cups hot cooked fettuccini
1½ cups baby artichokes
2 tablespoons extra virgin olive oil
1 cup smoked ham, cut into thin strips
2 tablespoons chopped shallots
1 teaspoon chopped garlic
1 cup chicken stock
2 tablespoons chopped ripe olives
2 tablespoons chopped green olives
¼ cup grated Parmesan cheese

Cooking utensils you'll need:
skillet
large stockpot
saucepan with cover
measuring cups
measuring spoons

Directions:

Use the large stockpot to cook the fettuccini according to package directions. Cook prepared (see "Tip") baby artichokes in boiling water in the saucepan until tender. Drain and cut them into bite-sized chunks. Put the olive oil in the skillet and sauté the ham, shallots, and garlic until the shallots are just tender. Add the chicken stock. As soon as it comes to a boil, add the fettuccini and artichokes. When the artichokes are hot, sprinkle with olives and Parmesan cheese and serve.

Tip:

Artichokes can seem mysterious and cooking with them can be a little intimidating at first. Most people love their savory, nut-like flavor, however, and find that cooking and eating them can be a lot of fun. After purchasing artichokes, sprinkle them with a few drops of water and store them in a plastic bag in your refrigerator until you want to use them. Before cooking, wash them and trim off the lower portion of the stem. Pull off any tough lower petals then continue snapping off just the tips of petals, leaving the edible bottom part of the petals on the artichoke, until you reach petals that have a paler green color. Cut the top off of the artichoke, and cut out the center petals and fuzzy center. You should be left with the "heart" of the artichoke and the edible portion of the leaves. Depending on the size of the artichoke, you may want to cut the heart lengthwise before cooking.

California Food History

Artichokes were first brought to California by the Spanish, and almost all commercially grown artichokes in the United States now come from California, where they contribute nearly $50 million to the annual economy. Monterey County accounts for approximately eighty percent of that yield, so in 1986 it was named "the Official Vegetable of Monterey" by the County Board of Supervisors.

This "fancy thistle" is a member of the sunflower family and a native of the Mediterranean. When you eat an artichoke, you are actually eating a flower bud. If the flowers are allowed to bloom, the beautiful violet-blue blossoms can measure seven inches across in diameter. The largest flower buds form at the top of central stems, while smaller ones are produced lower, and "baby artichokes" appear at the bottom.

Paella

Ingredients:

8 chicken legs
3 chorizo sausages, cut into 1-inch pieces
¾ cup extra virgin olive oil
1½ cups chopped onion
2 garlic cloves, chopped
½ cups medium-grain rice, uncooked
1 teaspoon salt
½ teaspoon white pepper
4 cups chicken stock (or 2 cups chicken stock and 2 cups clam juice)
1 teaspoon saffron (see "Tips")
1 pound shrimp, shelled and cleaned
1 tablespoon chopped parsley
½ cup white cooking wine
½ pound fresh clams, mussels, or both (washed but still in their shells, see "Tips")
2 cans artichoke hearts, drained
1 or 2 jars pimentos, drained
1 cup cooked peas
8 lobster or crab claws
2 lemons, quartered

Cooking utensils you'll need:
paella pan (paellera) or large, flat-bottomed pan
that is about 5 inches high
saucepan
mixing bowl
measuring cups
measuring spoons

Directions:

Pour ½ cup olive oil and wine into the mixing bowl. Add half of the garlic, half of the onions, and the parsley. Place the shrimp in this liquid and marinate in the refrigerator for at least an hour.

Meanwhile, pour 4 tablespoons olive oil into the paella pan and add sausage

and chicken. Cook over medium heat, turning the meat as necessary to brown all sides. Add the remaining garlic and onions and cook until they begin to brown. Remove meat, pour rice into the pan, and cook just until it begins to change color, stirring as necessary to keep the rice from burning.

Pour the chicken stock into the saucepan, bring it to a boil, and add saffron. Add salt and white pepper to the rice, pour the stock over it, stir, and place the sausage and chicken on top of the rice. Cover and cook over low heat just until the stock is absorbed by the rice.

Discard the marinade and lay the shrimp on top of the sausage and chicken. Layer the clams or mussels, lobster or crab legs, artichoke hearts, pimentos, and peas in the pan. Cover and cook over low heat for about 20 minutes. (Low heat is necessary since the rice is not stirred and you do not want it to burn.) Garnish with lemon slices and serve.

Tips:

High-quality paella pans conduct heat evenly across the bottom. If you don't have this type of pan, you need a large heat source to cover the entire bottom of your pan. That's one reason why many people make paella by placing the pan on a barbecue grill.

If you can't find chorizo sausage in your supermarket, you can substitute another type.

Wash clams and mussels well before cooking. Discard any with cracked shells. Those with open shells should close when placed in cold water. If they don't, test them by gently touching the interior with a knife. If they don't close, discard them. Mussels can be very sandy, so soak and swish them around in salted water, changing the water as needed. Pull off their beards and scrape off any barnacles.

California Food History and Food Facts

Originating in Spain, paella is one of the most impressive one-pot-meals ever invented and is most often reserved for special occasions. It is easy to see why people living in a coastal area such as California would like to make this food, as it features many different types of fresh seafood along with meats. You may want to make the preparation of this unique dish a family affair.

Saffron is actually the dried stigma of the saffron flower. This is the part of the pistil that receives pollen grains during fertilization. Each saffron flower has only three stigmas, so it takes approximately 75,000 flowers to make a single pound of saffron! Add to that the fact that the stigmas must be picked by hand and you end up with the most expensive spice in the world. In fact, saffron can cost more per ounce than gold! That's why only a very small amount is usually placed in spice jars. Saffron is traditional in this dish, and it imparts a unique flavor and lovely yellow-orange color to rice, but your paella will be delicious, even if you make it without this ingredient.

Chinese Almond Cookies

Ingredients:

1 cup butter or margarine
¾ cup sugar
1 egg
¾ cup ground blanched almonds
1 teaspoon almond extract
2½ cups flour
1½ teaspoons baking powder
dash salt
36 whole almonds
egg yolk

Cooking utensils you'll need:
food processor
2 mixing bowls
measuring cups
measuring spoons
cookie sheet
basting brush

Directions:

Grind the blanched almonds in a food processor, and measure the amount needed after grinding.

Place the butter in the bowl, add sugar and cream them together until mixture is light and fluffy. Add the egg and mix again. Stir in the almond extract and ground almonds and set aside. Combine the flour, baking powder and salt in the second bowl. Dump them into the first mixture and stir well. Form the mixture into a large ball, adding a little flour if it is too sticky, and place it in the refrigerator for 1 hour.

Preheat oven to 350° Fahrenheit, and remove the dough from the refrigerator. Using about a tablespoon of dough for each cookie, shape the dough into 1-inch balls. Place the dough balls on the cookie sheet, flatten them a bit with your hand, and press a whole almond on each one. Beat the egg yolk and brush a little onto each cookie. Bake for 20 to 25 minutes.

California Food History

Franciscan monks first planted almond trees in coastal areas of California in the 1700s. Unfortunately, the trees did not thrive in this moist area. An entire century passed before almond trees were successfully established farther inland. Many of the best-known varieties available today were developed during breeding programs back in the 1870s.

Almonds provide a good source of heart-healthy monounsaturated fat. They also contain vitamin E (an antioxidant), magnesium, riboflavin, phosphorus, and copper.

The discovery of gold at Sutter's Mill started the California Gold Rush, bringing many people from all over the world, including immigrants from China. Still more Chinese came to work on the western portion of the transcontinental railroad. Today, Chinese Americans are a rich and vital part of California culture. Their foods and flavors add unique dishes to the cuisine of this state.

Strawberry Cobbler

Ingredients:

Topping
1¾ cups flour
2 tablespoons white sugar
½ teaspoon salt
1 tablespoon baking powder
8 tablespoons cold butter
¾ cup milk
2 tablespoons brown sugar

Filling
2 quarts strawberries
1 cup sugar
⅓ cup flour
½ cup water
3 tablespoons lemon juice

Cooking utensils you'll need:
food processor or pastry blender
2 mixing bowls
measuring cups
measuring spoons
9x13-inch glass baking dish

Directions:

Put 13⁄4 cups flour, 2 tablespoons white sugar, 1 teaspoon salt, and the baking powder in a bowl or food processor and stir. Cut in 6 tablespoons of the cold butter until the mixture looks pebbly. Mix in the milk and form the dough into a ball. Chill in the refrigerator.

After about 30 minutes, preheat the oven to 400 degrees Fahrenheit. Mix 1 cup sugar with 1⁄3 cup flour. Stir in the water and lemon juice. Mix in the strawberries. Pour into the baking dish. Bake for about 15 minutes. Remove from heat and stir. Use your hands to drop small amounts of dough (about the size of a half dollar) on top of the filling. (Be careful not to burn yourself on the hot baking dish.) Using the remaining 2 tablespoons of butter, drop little chunks on top of the cobbler. Sprinkle with the brown sugar and return to the oven for another 30 minutes (until the dough is golden brown).

Tip:

Make this cobbler using any berries that are in season. Strawberries are a particularly healthy choice because they have only 50 calories per serving and more vitamin C than an orange!

California Food History

The great-great-great-great grandparents of today's strawberry come from two different continents—North America and South America. In the 1500s, explorers brought one of the grandparents back to France from Virginia. The Virginia fruit got people's attention because it had larger fruit and a deeper red color than the European strawberries of that time. And it produced more berries. But it had to wait nearly two hundred years for the other grandparent to arrive from South America.

In the early 1700s, a French spy noticed some really big strawberries in Chile while he was making maps of Spanish forts. He brought a bunch of them back to France. But they didn't reproduce in France. All the plants from Chile were female and needed pollen from other strawberry plants to produce fertile seeds. Once they were planted next to the strawberry plants from Virginia, they started producing fruit—and a new strawberry was born.

Today, California grows about three-fourths of U.S. strawberries. They can trace their ancestry back to the marriage of the Virginia and Chile strawberry in Europe 250 years ago.

Fig Cake

Preheat oven to 350 degrees Fahrenheit.

Ingredients:

4 egg whites
3 cups plus 2 tablespoons flour
4 teaspoons baking powder
½ teaspoon salt
1½ cups sugar
¾ cup butter
1 cup milk
1 teaspoon lemon flavoring
1 teaspoon cinnamon
1 tablespoon molasses
1½ cups chopped figs

Cooking utensils you'll need:
electric mixer
rubber spatula
3 mixing bowls
measuring cups
measuring spoons
bundt pan

Directions:

Grease and lightly flour the bundt pan.

Separate the whites from the yolks of the eggs. It's best to separate each egg into a small bowl and then pour it into the mixing bowl before separating the next egg to be certain that no yolk gets into the whites. If any yolk gets into the white part of the eggs, they will not turn bright white or get fluffy when you beat them.

Use the electric mixer to beat the egg whites until they are bright white and can stand in fluffy peaks. Set them aside.

Dredge figs in 2 tablespoons flour and set aside.

In a second mixing bowl, cream the sugar and butter. Blend in the milk and set aside.

In the third mixing bowl, mix the remaining flour, baking powder, and salt. Pour half of this into the butter/sugar mixture and beat well. Using the rubber spatula, fold in the beaten egg whites, then gently add the remaining flour and lemon flavoring. Pour 1/3 back into one of the empty bowls and set aside.

To the remaining mixture, add cinnamon, molasses, and figs. It will become darker than the mixture you set aside. Pour the darker mixture into the bundt pan. Add the lighter mixture and swirl it a bit with the rubber spatula to get a nice blend of colors. Bake for about 55 minutes. Cool for about 30 minutes, invert a plate on top of the cake pan, and turn the plate and pan over to release the cake.

California Food History

We can thank Spanish priests for first planting fig trees at the San Diego Mission in 1759. The process was repeated as each new mission was established. This historic association between missions and figs even led to naming California's leading black variety the Mission Fig. A popular golden-brown type, the Calimyrna Fig, had its origin in Turkey and was first planted in California in 1882. Figs were a food source for human beings much earlier than the eighteenth century, however. The first written documentation of figs appears in a book dating to about 2000 B.C. Later, the Greek King Mithridates ordered his subjects to eat figs every day because he believed they were an antidote for all sickness. Early Olympic athletes used them as a training food, and they were presented to honor winners of the games. Today, California's Central Valley is the source of all dried figs that are commercially harvested in the United States. Figs are an excellent source of both soluble and insoluble fiber. They also contain a significant amount of calcium, iron, potassium, and antioxidants.

Further Reading

Brown, Carrie and John Werner. *The Jimtown Store Cookbook: Recipes from Sonoma County's Favorite Country Market*. New York: HarperCollins, 2002.

Comfort, Mary, Noreen Griffee, and Charlene Walker, eds. *California Artichoke Cookbook*. Berkeley, Calif.: Celestial Arts, 1998.

James, Sally. *Escape to Yountville: Recipes for Health and Relaxation from Napa Valley*. Berkeley, Calif.: Ten Speed Press, 2003.

Jordan, Michele Anna. *California Home Cooking: American Home Cooking in the California Style*. Boston, Mass: The Harvard Common Press, 1997.

Jordan, Michele Anna. *San Francisco Seafood: Savory Recipes from Everybody's Favorite Seafood City*. Berkeley, Calif.: Ten Speed Press, 2001.

Mansfield, Leslie. *Asian Pasta (Recipes from the Vineyards of Northern California)*. Berkeley, Calif.: Celestial Arts, 2000.

Michael, Chiarello. *Napa Stories: Profiles, Reflections, and Recipes from the Napa Valley*. New York: Stewart, Tabori & Chang, 2001.

Pinedo, Encarnacion. *Encarnacion's Kitchen: Mexican Recipes from Nineteenth-Century California*. Berkeley and Los Angeles, Calif.: University of California Press, 2003.

Pritchard, Gwen, Alice Waters, and Gina Gallo, eds. *California Fresh Harvest: A Seasonal Journey through Northern California*. Oakland, Calif.: Junior League of Oakland-East Bay, Inc., 2001.

Rodgers, Judy R. and Gerald Asher. *The Zuni Café Cookbook: A Compendium of Recipes and Cooking Lessons from San Francisco's Beloved Restaurant*. New York: W.W. Norton & Company, 2002.

Schroeder, Lisa Golden. *California Gold Rush Cooking (Exploring History Through Simple Recipes)*. Blue Earth Books, 2001.

For More Information

California History
www.californiahistory.net

California Picnic Recipes
www.alanskitchen.com/picnicking/state_menu/California.html

Caribbean Recipes
www.calantilles.com/rindex.html

Fresh Produce and Meat Recipes with Nutritional Information
www.cafecreosote.com/Recipes/category_index.php3?cat=California%20Cuisine

Publisher's note:
The Web sites listed on this page were active at the time of publication. The publisher is not responsible for Web sites that have changed their addresses or discontinued operation since the date of publication. The publisher will review and update the Web sites upon each reprint.

Index

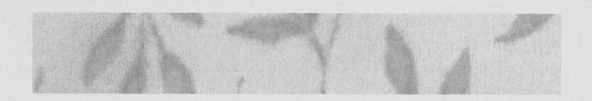

Index

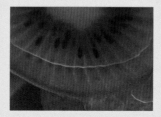

Author:

In addition to writing, Joyce Libal has worked as an editor for a half dozen magazines, including a brief stint as recipe editor at *Vegetarian Gourmet*. Most of her experience as a cook, however, has been gained as the mother of three children and occasional surrogate mother to several children from different countries and cultures. She is an avid gardener and especially enjoys cooking with fresh herbs and vegetables and with the abundant fresh fruit that her husband grows in the family orchard.

Recipe Tester / Food Preparer:

Bonni Phelps owns How Sweet It Is Café in Vestal, New York. Her love of cooking and feeding large crowds comes from her grandmothers on both sides whom also took great pleasure in large family gatherings.

Consultant:

The Culinary Institute of America is considered the world's premier culinary college. It is a private, not-for-profit learning institution, dedicated to providing the world's best culinary education. Its campuses in New York and California provide learning environments that focus on excellence, leadership, professionalism, ethics, and respect for diversity. The institute embodies a passion for food with first-class cooking expertise.

Recipe Contributor:

Patricia Therrien has worked for several years with Harding House Publishing Service as a researcher and recipe consultant—but she has been experimenting with food and recipes for the past thirty years. Her expertise has enriched the lives of friends and family. Patty lives in western New York State with her family and numerous animals, including several horses, cats, and dogs.

Picture Credits

Cover: Benjamin Stewart, Photos.com, Photos.com. P. 9: Photos.com. P. 10: Photos.com. P. 12: Photos.com. P. 15: PhotoDisc, Benjamin Stewart, Benjamin Stewart, Benjamin Stewart, Photos.com, Photos.com, Benjamin Stewart, Benjamin Stewart. P. 16: Benjamin Stewart, Benjamin Stewart, Benjamin Stewart, Benjamin Stewart, Photos.com, Benjamin Stewart, Benjamin Stewart, Benjamin Stewart, Photos.com, Benjamin Stewart. P. 18: Photos.com, Benjamin Stewart, Benjamin Stewart, Benjamin Stewart, Benjamin Stewart, Benjamin Stewart, Benjamin Stewart, Benjamin Stewart. P. 19: Benjamin Stewart. P. 20: Benjamin Stewart. P. 21: Photos.com. P. 22: Photos.com. P. 24: Benjamin Stewart. P. 25: Benjamin Stewart. P. 27: Benjamin Stewart. P. 29: PhotoDisc. P. 37: Benjamin Stewart. P. 38: Benjamin Stewart. P. 41: BrandX. P. 43: Benjamin Stewart. P. 45: PhotoDisc. P. 47: PhotoDisc. P. 48: Photos.com. P. 51: Benjamin Stewart. P. 54: PhotoDisc. P. 57: PhotoDisc. P. 60: Photos.com. P. 61: PhotoDisc. P. 62: PhotoDisc. P. 64: Photos.com. P. 68: Photos.com, PhotoDisc, Photos.com. P. 69: Photos.com, PhotoDisc, Photos.com. P. 27: Photos.com.